DEVIL'S LETHAL DOSE

DEVIL'S LETHAL DOSE

Are You Not Deceived

Rev. Lukas Utete

Dip. Theo., BA. Theo

To order additional copies of this book, contact:
Xlibris Corporation
0-800-644-6988
www.xlibrispublishing.co.uk
Orders@xlibrispublishing.co.uk
304848

CONTENTS

ABSTRACT

This book is written to emphasise the fact that salvation is through the finished work of the cross of Jesus Christ and that there is only one God who is almighty and eternal who revealed himself through the person of Jesus Christ.

It looks at the various ways the devil is deceiving people into believing that there are many ways of reaching God. It tries to highlight the danger that is in taking false teaching because any other means of worship apart from through Jesus Christ does not lead to the one true God but to a god which is devil worship.

It touches on the fall of man, that man was created being allergic to sin. The writer then touches in brief how Jesus Christ touched him.

Then the great deception is revealed through the Bible and proof is given why Bible must be believed as the holy true infallible word of God.

The writer then looks at the purpose of Mosaic Law and why it was not intended to impart salvation. He also explains that one cannot choose a part of the Mosaic Law like keeping of the Sabbath without taking the whole law book, and he then explains who Jesus Christ is, the Holy Spirit, and God the father and explains what is meant by the *finished* work of the cross.

Unless stated, most quotations are from King James Version.

ACKNOWLEDGEMENTS

I dedicate this book to my lovely dear wife Maria who carried the burden of looking after the family and providing for the family and for my college fees during my years at Bible College. I thank her for enduring the many sleepless nights she had when I woke up to write or put ideas that flooded my mind down on paper.

I also dedicate it to my children Blessing, Tapiwa, and Tendai who did typing of the final corrections. To Blessing, I thank you for assisting your mother during those difficult times. You sacrificed a lot.

I give my thanks to Dr C. M. Murefu, Principal of Living Waters Bible College, who taught me in my third year and my fourth year degree program. He challenged me in his talk on 'Managing Ideas'. Many of his insights are included in this book. Thank you, sir.

I give thanks to Living Waters Bible College Faculty with special thanks to Rev. Ron Johnson.

I thank Mrs Fortunate Nyakudya for typing and Miss Fortune Gwafa and Mr Nelson Nyamandi for assisting with typing and making corrections. Many thanks to Miss Doroty Chigwenhese who organised the typing and follow-ups and encouraged the typist and kept on challenging me to finish the book which she had read five times before publication.

Finally, many thanks to Apostolic Faith Mission in Zimbabwe, Tomlinson Depot Assembly, who encouraged me to write a book of what I had taught them in our Bible Studies.

CHAPTER 1

Where Do You Stand?

I start to write this book because of the burden that the Holy Spirit has put in my heart. God has given me an opportunity to see devious ways of operating of the master deceiver who is very cunning. He is the devil. I am not going to argue for the existence of the devil, but I am looking at his operations. If one does not believe in the existence of the devil, I urge such a person to examine what is happening in his or her own respective society and make his own conclusions.

The devil is the supreme spirit of evil, a superhuman malignant being whose aim and focus is to destroy anything that is good and in honour of the almighty God who is,
'the creator of all things: . . . in heaven and that are in earth, visible and invisible . . .' (Col. 1: 16, KJV)

In passing, let me say if people do not believe in the existence of God, why then is it that of all the species on earth it is only humans who ask questions pertaining to where we came from, why are we here, and where we are going? If it's true that God does not exist and if our minds cannot imagine and name a thing that does not exist, how did our minds come to think of God? We know that there are things that had not been discovered some hundreds of years ago, and before discovery no one knew about them, but when they were discovered, they were given names. In that trend of thought, people know deep down that there is God but through devil's influence decide to reject Him and hide under pretext that He does not exist. God has given special revelation of Himself through the Bible and general revelation of Himself through creation.

> Because that which may be known of God is Manifest in them:
> For God had shewed it unto them. For the visible things of Him
> from Creation of the world are clearly seen, being understood by the
> things that are made, even His eternal power and Godhead; so that
> they are without excuse. (Rom. 1: 19-20, KJV)

Man can only sin against God who is the absolute standard of right and wrong. Why is it that even atheists who believe there is no God say it's bad and evil when someone steals from them? How can there be evil if the devil does not exist and how can man speak of good and bad if God does not exist?

In every society, people do not condone killing of other beings, why? I believe it is because man was created in the image of God and because of the law that God put and wrote in our conscience we uphold the sanctity of life. Lions do not feel guilty if they kill another animal for food. Even other wild animals do not feel guilty if they kill one of their kinds in fighting for territorial supremacy, why? They are not created in the image of God, and they do not have conscience. Let me on this chapter finish by starting the *wager* argument which says, 'One should choose to believe and trust in God because if He exists you win everything and if He does not exist you lose nothing so believe and be safe.' Do not be deceived and follow the world which says, show me and I believe: God says, 'believe and I will show you'. Faith must be the starting point.

> But without faith it is impossible to please him: for he that cometh
> to God must believe that He is, and that He is a rewarder of them
> that diligently seek Him. (Heb. 11: 6, KJV)

It is important that people should not live like animals but must examine their lives and be convinced of the true purpose of their being here and be sure of where they came from and are going. According to Greek philosophers, the ignorant man cannot be genuinely happy. Socrates' maxim, 'The unexamined life is not worth living,' is important to note, also we need to take not of what was central in the writings of two greatest Greek philosophers Plato and Aristotle who quoted, 'to know the good is to do it.' If one is not sure of his origin, he or she cannot be happy. If one does not examine his life, it leads to poor self-image, uncertainty, lack of interest in life, which leads to stress and its consequence. Examine yourself; know God and do good, you will enjoy this life and life to come. Do not think being in the church means you are saved. You must be born-again. Read on to find out how.

CHAPTER 2

Fall of Man

You may be depressed and have tried everything possible, but there seems to be no help anywhere. It could be you are battered day in day out by your husband. He always tells you that he loves you and after battering he pleads to you not to leave him but he loses it again when he gets drunk. You may have tried the psychic, the psychologist, and a church but because even your local priest cannot help you, you are contemplating suicide; somebody loves you so much that he died for you, his name is Jesus Christ. Please read this book through before you kill yourself. Jesus understands your problem more than you think. Give him a chance after all what do you lose you have been to all sources and people, he is your last chance. All the hatred, jealously, pain, hurt, and killing in the world is as a result of man's fall. God gave clear specific instructions to Adam.

> Of every tree of the garden thou mayest freely eat: but of the tree of
> the knowledge of good and evil, thou shalt not eat of it: for in the
> day that thou eatest thereof thou shall surely die. (Gen. 2: 16-17)

The devil is still using the same method of causing man to fall. He uses only three things as it is said in the Bible.

> Love not the world. If any man love the world, the love of the father
> is not in him. For all that is in the world, the lust of the flesh, and
> the lust of the eyes, and the pride of life, is not of the father, but is of
> the world. (1 John 2: 15-16, KJV)

We note in the fall of man in Eden Garden the same method.

> And when the woman saw that the tree was *good for food* and that it
> was *pleasant to the eyes*, and a tree to be *desired to make man wise*, she
> took of the tree thereof, and did eat, and gave also unto her husband
> with her, and he did eat. (Gen. 3: 6, KJV)

Note that 'good for food' is lust of the flesh. 'Pleasant to the eyes' is lust of
the eyes, and 'desired to make one wise' is the pride of life. We also note here
that Eve who had been seeing this tree all along was only able to see these
things about the tree when the devil spoke to here. Watch out when you listen
to him speak to you. When he speaks, attack back by the word of God as Jesus
did when he was tempted of the devil in Matthew 4: 1-11.

We also note here that in this scripture verse it is said Adam was 'with her',
which means he heard the whole conversation but did not use the word of God
to stop the devil. He is the master of deception who knows which words to use
to cast doubt in your belief.

> Yea, hath God said Ye shall not eat of *every* tree of the garden?
> (Gen. 3: 1)

The word cunningly used here is *'every'* so even Adam started to doubt
whether he had heard correctly what God had said; therefore, he kept quiet
and failed in his role to protect his wife as a husband.

Today, many husbands do not want to worship the true God but allow
their wives to go and worship wherever they want, as a result some women
have been deceived into false religions because the husband is not there to
protect her. Some husbands are even protected from evil by their wives who
are true born-again children of God. In Africa where Apostolic sects have
mushroomed, some wives are taken as wives by these false prophets as the
women go to seek for treatment or cleansing from the so-called 'man of god',
but the painful thing is that the husband will be busy doing something or
drinking beer. Husbands including pastors must have a relationship with God
through Jesus Christ so that they can be first and foremost priests to their
families. God will hold every husband accountable of the spirituality of his
family.

Watch out you fathers when your children watch devilish films on TV and
bring pornographic materials home.

Some fathers say they are respecting their daughter's privacy by not entering
the daughter's bedroom not knowing that there is someone entering her
bedroom through these materials from the occult world. It is your responsibility

to screen what your children see and read. Do it in love and explain why it is not good for them. Read the Bible with them.

Man was created by God to dominate, subdue, and rule God's creation, but he failed because of the fall. Man has through pride exalted himself and refused to worship his creator and decided to provoke God by worshiping a creature which was created. When man listened to the devil and obeyed him, man lost his position of authority and rulership to creature. Because of the fall, man no longer knows the purpose why God created him. Man now worships snakes, baboons, monkeys, and idols made from wood and stone all things God created for man to dominate. Man gave legal right to the devil to control his life when he fell in Eden Garden.

The enemy is drunk with human blood and is obsessed by the idea of becoming like God. Therefore, the devil uses any method to get people to worship him as they do to God. He has therefore followed people in churches to cunningly draw them away from the true God to worship devil without them knowing it. He is using false religion and false doctrine as his lethal dose. I am here to unveil his plans and methods. I pray that you will seriously take note and stock of your life as you prayerfully read this book.

CHAPTER 3

Man Allergic to Sin

'Many people suffer from allergies which is severe physical reaction to such allergen as pollen, dust, foods, feathers, insect venom, animal dander and medications. Anaphylactic shock is the most severe form of allergic reaction. It can develop in minutes or even seconds after contact with allergen or it may appear half an hour or more later or even progress suddenly from an apparently mild allergic reaction. The face, chest and back become flushed, itchy and burning: skin rashes may appear. The face, tongue and lips may swell and the lips turn bluish. Breathing is labored and wheezing. The pulse becomes weak, pale skin; dizziness, nausea and headache may follow. Finally, the person may lapse into coma'.[1]

(According to a publication in Reader's Digest entitled, 'Practical Problem Solver'. page 10.)

In the church today are many people who have lapsed into spiritual coma. As a person in coma does not know what hit him and is unable to help himself so is the one in spiritual coma. They don't know they are in coma and what caused it. They are now so used to their situation that they consider it normal. Man was created by God being allergic to sin.

For the wages of sin is death: but the gift of God is eternal life through Jesus Christ our Lord. (Rom. 6: 23)

Once man sins, he automatically dies spiritually, but physically he goes on living but is now facing the world and the ravaging effects of weather. The devil no longer stops people who want to go to church, but they go on his ticket which has prescription of how they must worship. He has established his own gatherings called 'churches' but not the true God's Church of the called out ones from darkness to light and life where the emphasis is god not Jesus but one wonders which God. God I know has revealed himself through Jesus. I have called this 'lethal dose' because just as a patient calmly waits while a nurse administers an injection in his veins in a belief that it's going to help cure the illness and speed up recover. But, unfortunately, if he is allergic to the drug, it may do the very opposite and kill him instead of giving him more days on this earth.

Lethal dose is the amount of a toxic compound or drug that causes death in humans or animals. It is very important that we expose the devil's method.

When you go to war, it is very essential to plant specialised spies to study the strength of the enemy, the weapons, methods of fighting, and then relay that information to base so offensive and defensive plans can be formulated. For our war, we don't need to send people to the devil to learn because our God is omniscient which means he knows all and reveals it to his people as and when he sees necessary. Here we are giving each other information about the weapons and fighting strategies of the enemy. This information must help you withstand him.

We have people in churches who are not sure of their salvation. Some stay on because they are shy to be seen to have backslidden yet they actually have. In Zimbabwe, we used to use passbook for savings especially with building societies. If you had withdrawn all your money, they would not take the passbook from you, which do not mean that you had money. The passbook would be cancelled and given back to you. You could even go into the queue for withdrawals for nobody would ask if you had money in your account or not. You could even chart with other people in the queue waiting to withdraw from their accounts, but eventually, your time would come and the sad information you receive would be 'Sorry no funds'. Then you would walk out empty-handed, disappointed, and ashamed. This is what is happening with many people who have not invested their lives with Jesus Christ. They may go to church, pay tithes and offerings, be in the choir, even be promoted to be an elder, or go to Bible college and become a pastor, but all this happens because you are in the queue of life. Eventually, the day will come when your turn arrives and you die only to be told 'No Life'. For the scriptures says,

> He that hath the Son hath life: and he that hath not the Son of God hath not life. (1 John 5: 12, KJV)

It is also important to note that if you are a motor vehicle driver and you drive recklessly or without due care and attention and as a result you cause accident that kills people. If your licence is cancelled, what is taken from you is *the authority to drive but the ability to drive remains.* This maybe what some people are, they go to church, they carry Bibles, they preach, pay tithes and give offerings, yet licence to enter Heaven has been withdrawn.

This happens to those who were once saved and born-again but have allowed the devil to speak to them and lead them away from faith. Such remain with a form of godliness but have denied the power as it is said in 2 Timothy 3: 5.

If you take a cup full of poison and drink, you die. On the other hand, if you put 5 per cent of the deadly poison in a cup filled with 95 per cent full of water, you still die. Death is not caused because of the quantity but because of the deadliness of the poison. The devil by allowing people to go to churches is happy if they have 95 per cent truth and 5 per cent lies because he knows it will all be lies. Take an example of a jar full of raspberry. If you pour in some water till it's full, it will still be red. It does not change to be like water. If you then take a glass of clean water half-full and pour a bit of raspberry, you see though the glass is not full but the little bit of red raspberry added will cause the whole glass contents to turn red.

The same goes with lies; if you have truth and lies is added, it is all lies. If a sinner is told the sound biblical doctrine and does not accept Holy Spirit conviction that he or she is a sinner, the knowledge becomes head knowledge which puffs up but cannot lead one to salvation. So how does the devil mix lies and truth? We will see in the next chapter.

CHAPTER 4

Are You Not Deceived?

One of devil's lethal doses is that there are many ways to reach God. All earthly religions talk of some god somewhere. This started long back when man stated humanism at the Tower of Babel (Gen. 11); man wanted to be free from God, be independent of Him, and do what they wanted. Even today man wants to be free to worship the way he wants and to a god he wants. Man now speaks of 'Human Rights'. They say for God to say that we must worship Him alone and through Jesus Christ is unfair. They forget that God is not fair but just. The devil knows very well that he cannot change what God has said. *If God accepted any way to come to Him as acceptable and true, true it must have been ordained by Him; therefore, there was no need for Him to send his son to die for mankind if means to reach God were there.* "Nevertheless, even if it were true, which it is not, when God sent his son, He cancelled any other means."

> God, who at sundry times and divers manners spoke in time past unto the fathers by the prophets. Hath in these last days spoken unto us by his son, whom he hath appointed heir of all things, by whom also he made the worlds. (Heb. 1: 1-2, KJV)

It is futile to hold on to one's own religion which has its own way of reaching to God apart from what the almighty has stated. The devil also is teaching people that if one receives Christ as Lord and Saviour, he must work either through tithing, offering, helping the needy, fasting, or so on to *complete the salvation*. I am not saying these are bad. I am only looking at the motive. Some of the things that were done by Pharisees were good, but the motive was bad, therefore they were not accepted by God. Some Jews followed Paul in Galatia and taught that they were supposed to keep ceremonial laws of Moses and be circumcised to complete their salvation. Paul saw the danger of this teaching because he knew that doctrinal error was more dangerous than moral error. If a person commits adultery, he can confess and be forgiven, but if a person believes a false doctrine, how can he repent when he believes that his belief will save him?

Therefore he does not even thank them as he does in his other epistles. The Judaisers (Jewish Christian believers who accepted Christ but with addition had to follow Mosaic Law as prerequisite for completion of salvation) did not believe in the finished work of the cross and felt obedience to Mosaic Law was necessary for salvation and added 'works' to Christ's work on the cross. This according to Paul nullified the effect of the power of the blood of Jesus.

These Christian Jews were in spiritual coma and did not know that what they were preaching was taking away salvation from people in exchange with death.

In Galatians 3: 12 (KJV), it is said,

> 'And the law is not of faith; but, the man that doeth them shall live in them.'

The principle here is you either go to God by Jesus Christ, righteousness, or your own, but they cannot mix. If you keep the law, find your whole existence by it full and totally. Keep the law perfectly. You cannot keep the law, but when you fail in some areas, you want to move to grace through faith. They cannot mix as they are like oil and water. "If you live by law, you will be judged by law." If you leave under grace through faith, you will be judged under that.

It is as if it's raining and you are under an umbrella. You cannot put another umbrella over the one you are in and expect that the second will protect you. It must be one umbrella at a time, but you must choose which one to take. You either accept the finished work of the Cross of Calvary where Jesus died for our sins or decide to go through Mosaic Law but you cannot mix the two.

> All who sin apart from the law will also perish apart from the law, and all who sin under the law will be judged by the law. For it is not those who hear the law who are righteous in God's sight but it is those who obey the law who will be declared righteous. (Rom. 2: 12-13, KJV)

There are some who want to keep Sabbath as the major thing to have salvation complete. This is another devil's 'lethal dose'. One cannot keep Sabbath and refuse to be circumcised because if you live by the law, you must live by it and keep the whole law, not some at your convenience. If one wants to keep the Sabbath in honour of God, there is no problem as long as one does not expect to be saved through his efforts of keeping the Day. Anything elevated to accord salvation to mankind apart from Jesus Christ is an insult to God who had to have His Son killed for people who had other ways of reaching Him.

> Behold, I Paul say unto you, that if ye be circumcised, Christ shall profit you nothing. For I testify again to every man that is circumcised, *that he is a debtor to do the whole law.* Christ is become of no effect unto you, whosoever of you are justified by the law, you are fallen from grace (Gal. 5: 2-4.)

If you decide to add to the finished work of the cross, you have decided to go to heaven by your own righteousness but God has rejected you before you even start because 'Our righteousness is like filthy rags before him' (Isa. 64: 6). Some may argue and say it was Paul's own personal desire because he had been preaching about justification by faith only but we get our confidence from scripture.

> All scripture is given by inspiration of God, and it is profitable for doctrine, for reproof, for correction, for instruction in righteousness. (2 Tim. 3: 16, KJV)

The keyword here is 'All' including what Paul wrote saying 'I Paul' was also inspired.

If you are circumcised, keep the whole law, and likewise, if you keep Sabbath, keep the whole law for you have a debt to keep it all. Way of law you cannot be justified because it's not the way of faith. Way of faith you are justified because of Jesus's righteousness. Whichever you choose, you live by it. The law is not faith, they are mutually exclusive. We tithe in love to our God not as a law to buy salvation or acceptance. Anything we do for the purpose of buying salvation or acceptance kills us spiritually. No one can help Jesus. Salvation is a complete package which needs no addition. The law can only condemn not justify.

> 'But that no man is justified by the law in the sight of God, it is evident: for, the just shall live by faith.' (Gal. 3: 11)

The law is an indivisible unity. If you want to keep it, the whole law is over your head; break one, you have broken all and penalty is death.

Sabbath was established as a day of rest, a *Holy Day* not a *Holiday*. The day was reserved for mutual fellowship and intimate communication with God. As a day of rest, it prefigured Christ who is our rest, our Sabbath.

> Come unto me, all ye that labour and are heavy laden, and I will give you *REST*. (Matt. 11: 28)

We rest in Christ, rest from worry, rest from anxiety, rest from sin, rest from torment by the devil, and so on.

Some have condemned those of us who have accepted and received Jesus as Lord and Saviour and understood that we cannot add to what Jesus did by keeping a day. Yet scripture teaches us that these ceremonies were a shadow.

> Let no man therefore judge you in . . . Respect of an Holy Day . . . of the Sabbath days: which are shadow of things to come; but the body of Christ. (Col. 2: 16-17, KJV)

I spoke to one brother who claimed to believe in Jesus but believed also that he had to keep the Sabbath to complete his salvation. I asked him if he was able to keep it exactly as was stipulated by God in Old Testament. He told me that he was not able to every week because things were difficult in Zimbabwe and therefore, God would understand. You see how devil deceives people. In Old Testament times, to break the law meant death; there was no room for explaining why you broke the law. Why are such people not killed? It's because of grace that was brought by Christ, but they still believe he did not complete the work of redemption.

The Purpose of the Law

Galatians 3: 19-25

1. Restrain and expose sin and not to impart life.
2. It was a temporary measure until the seed came
3. It was inferior because mediators were used (Angels to represent God—Moses to represent the people). Promise to Abraham involved a direct channel between God and Man.
4. It was a means of condemnation locking all under sin so that man's foundation could be seen for what it is—totally futile.
5. It was a tutor to lead us to Christ that we might be justified by faith. Now that faith has come we are no longer under the supervision of the law (or disciplinarian until Christ come.)

6. It was a temporary measure for a temporary purpose.
7. It was ordained of God; therefore, it could not be in conflict with the promise or Christ.
8. To show our inability and failure to keep the law.

The devil is leading people in Churches, especially in Africa, by teaching people that God helps those who help themselves. The God I know does not want people to be independent of him but dependent so he says:

> Trust in the Lord with all thine heart; and lean not unto thine own understanding. In all thy ways acknowledge Him, and He shall direct thy paths. (Prov. 3: 5)

When the devil attacks those in search of help, he wants people to focus on his instructions of 'healing' through 'false prophets' and n'angas or witch doctors. Devil knows when people do that they are worshipping him not God. I have heard people say that there is a man of god who only prays for water and does not touch herbs or charms. These people use marine spirits and familiar spirits as just one of the many other devil's departments set up to deceive people.

The devil also is taking away the fear of God from people as a result our churches are full of professional actors and not Christians. They move around with marks on their faces written 'Christian', but they only act Christianity. People should know that law demanded righteousness which it could not give. Grace did not abolish the law, but fulfilled the law.

Christ is the completeness of all that was intended by the law. He grants power over sin, which the law could not. Turn to Jesus who removes fear.

'For God has not given us a spirit of fear, but of power and of love and of sound mind.' (2 Tim. 1: 7)

Christianity is a relationship with God. Many people fear a pastor and other fellow Christians than they do God. The danger is that one day the mask will be taken off and it will be said the one who was acting as so and so is so and so and judgment will be pronounced, 'I never knew you'. We now have sinners in church disguised in suits. The suit I refer to is either church uniform, or being a member of a church denomination or being active and having a position of leadership in any church. If you have no personal relationship with God through the finished work of the cross and the shed blood of Jesus Christ by accepting him as Lord and Saviour, you are in a suit disguised as a Christian yet you are not. "You are playing church." But the devil knows his and God knows His.

'Nevertheless, God's solid foundation stands firm sealed with this inscription: The Lord knows those who are his' (2 Tim. 2: 19; CF Num. 16: 5, NIV)

One may feel is disguised to people but God knows and the devil knows. It is like at a manufacturing firm when employees come to work and go home it's impossible to tell who works in which department because they will be in their own clothes. But when they change into overalls, some say in yellow overalls for production department, some red for sales department, some blue for warehouse, and so on. It's easy to say by colour who works in which department. More still most companies write the department at the back of the overall. One read Production Department, Sales Department, or Warehouse department on the back of the employees. May I ask what name is written behind your back which is invisible to the naked eye but visible to spiritual eye? Is it written 'Born-Again' or 'Death'? Is the devil calling you his or Jesus is saying my child?

CHAPTER 5

At What Expense?

With much evangelism and general preaching of the gospel worldwide and the move of the Holy Spirit, millions are coming to the Lord and being baptised in the Holy Spirit. The devil who is the master copycat has come up with a copy of what God is doing. In Zimbabwe, where in African traditional religion, it is believed once a person dies, he or she is promoted to the level of accepting prayers from the living and passing them on to the next departed relative till the prayer reaches the Almighty God. In this religion, Jesus has no place.

It seems to our youth it's no longer fashionable to go to the witch doctors or n'angas who are the architects of methods, systems, and procedures of communicating with the spirits of the dead. The devil has given them a replacement with something acceptable and fashionable. He has set up churches that profess to preach the true gospel yet it's another gospel. Some even call the name Jesus, but when you closely look at the way they say 'In the name of Jesus', people are lured, especially when the preacher claim to heal the sick. People are not aware that Paul spoke about a Jesus apart from the one he preached. This is the spirit of 'another Jesus'.

> For if someone comes to you and preaches a Jesus other than the Jesus we preached, or if you receive a different spirit from the one you received, or a different gospel from the one you accepted . . . (2 Cor. 11: 4, NIV)

Some may even say if he is not true Jesus preached at our church, why is it that I was healed and I now have a prosperous business. Remember devil gives nothing for free. It is always in exchange for your soul after all when the devil offered all the kingdoms of the world to Jesus our Lord who created him or Lord did not argue or challenge him because he knew the devil as the god of this earth has control over them. (2 Corinthians 4: 4, Luke 4: 6 and Matthew 4: 9). From his control of kingdoms, he subdues them by his deception through signs and wonders.

> 'The coming of the lawless one will be like in accordance to with the work of satan displayed in all kinds of counterfeit miracles, signs and wonders.' (2 Thess. 2: 9, NIV)

We see then that the devil can heal and can even give wealth but at what expense? It must also be noted that it is the devil who cause poverty and diseases, so he cannot fail to remove what he has put in you. He does not give you healing because he is god but because he wants you to sink deep into his religion and then he will kill you. He has blinded the minds of those who believe his lies so that the light of the glorious gospel of Christ who is the image of God should not shine unto them. There are those who teach and preach a different gospel; it is the very same gospel preached by Paul but has something added to it which makes it different, so Paul warns against this.

> As we have already said, so now I say again: if anybody is preaching to you a gospel other than what you accepted, let him be eternally condemned. (Gal. 1: 9 NIV)

It is like if you have a jar of pure orange juice and if you add water to it, you no longer have pure orange juice and pure water. You have something new which I have no name for. This is happening when people take some aspects of African traditional religion which they think are dear to their hearts and want to mix them with Christianity. You end up with what is called syncretism—a mixture which is not African traditional religion but something new which God does not accept but the devil rejoices with because he knows with that belief one can never be saved. People forget that the devil does not always appear as a 'grotesque monster with horns, hoofs, forked tail, or a hobgoblin'. He at times appears as an angle of light (2 Cor. 11: 14).

I have heard people in these false religions quoting this scripture verse as they describe the work of the Holy Spirit and the speaking in other tongues. You can see how deep those people in devil's deception. They see evil as good and good as evil. They are so used to the devil and his evil ways that they believe it to be normal and true. Speaking in tongues they say it's demonic.

I have noted in rural areas during rainy season if a town dweller goes there, he can find people in the hut warming themselves over a fire made out from wet wood which emit a lot of smoke. From outside you cannot see people inside, but you can hear them chat and laugh. If the town dweller enters the hut, he cannot stay inside for more than five minutes. He comes out with tears in his eyes, mucus coming out, and coughing, why? He is not used to it, so is the same with people born-again and filled with Holy Spirit; when they enter such Churches, they come out quickly because it's uncomfortable to stay inside longer. However, there are the used ones whose conscience have been seared and rendered numb by the devil's sting, such people stay on oblivious of the warnings being given daily by the Holy Spirit through the preaching of the gospel. They believe the devil,

'Who changed the truth of God into a lie, and worshipped And served the creature more than the creator, Who is blessed forever.' (Rom. 1: 25, KJV)

'For such men are false apostles, deceitful workmen, masquerading as apostles of Christ. And no wonder, for satan himself masquerades as an angel of light. It is not surprising, then, if his servants masquerade as servants of righteousness. Their end will be what their actions deserve.' (2 Cor. 11: 13-15, NIV)

I have had some Christians say their guardian angels had come to help them and some even claim to have communicated with them. What puzzles me is the fact that some say they can pray to their guardian angel who can redeem them. How can an angel redeem us yet angels are spirits and have no blood?

'And without the shedding of blood there is no forgiveness.' (Heb. 9: 22, NIV)

'He did not enter by means of blood of goats and calves But he entered the most Holy Place once for all by his own blood, Having obtained eternal redemption' (Heb. 9: 12, NIV)

If Jesus Christ obtained our redemption once and for all, how can it be repeated through angels he created? For angels to give redemption, it means Jesus did not complete the work.

CHAPTER 6

He Touched Me

I had chronic headache and stomach pains for seventeen years. It became so severe that I did not want to speak because any movement I made, made it worse and any type of noise I heard increased my headache. Having gone to doctors and specialists and coming out every time with the pain, I decided to follow what other people were saying. I travelled throughout Zimbabwe to the remotest parts of our dearest country in search of witch doctors who I had heard to be popular and able to cure any type of disease.

I went to several witch doctors paying lots of money. Some suggested I brew opaque beer which I did to appease ancestral spirits, but it did not help. I then turned to apostolic sects to the so-called 'prophets'. At times we could go up the mountain and sleep there being prayed for. At times they could pray for milk and at times water which I was given to drink, but it did not help. One time, I was told to buy half dozen eggs, 500 ml milk, orange juice, and cooking oil. These things were mixed and after thorough stirring, the 'prophet' put some salt and gave me to drink. I vomited but the treatment only made my stomach problems worse.

There came a time when I seriously thought of committing suicide. I remember on three occasions as I drove from work going to *Chitungwiza* where I lived, I decided to drive into Hunyani River bridge to end the pain. Three times as I got to the bridge, I closed my eyes but somehow I could find myself on the other side of the bridge. Thank God for saving me; if not, I would be in hell right now.

I became more desperate and was then taking any advice I could get. It was at this time that I heard of a prominent spirit medium in Makonde area. I was told that he was so powerful that those who go for treatment at his place get healed as they alight from the bus at bus stop. It was said that many people had been heard testifying to this. I decided to go there. I was in terrible pain. The headache was so severe that to open eyes was like increasing the pain, the same with closing them. At least I had hope as was convinced that the trip I was taking was to be the journey I would never forget. With this thought in mind, I endured the pain all the way to this remote part of our dear country Zimbabwe. As I got closer, the gravel road we were using became more bumpy and the driver oblivious of the fact that he was carrying passengers increased the speed.

As we were jostled sideways, front, and backwards, I kept telling myself to cheer up as the problem was going to be over soon. Then the bus slowed down and the conductor shouted out the name of the station as the bus stopped. My headache had increased. I started to walk towards a small grass thatched hut on a hilltop. I was then beginning to wonder whether what I had heard was correct. As I walked in the field of this prominent spirit medium towards his village, the pain increased.

Finally, I arrived and was greeted by an old woman dressed in black. I was directed to a small hut at the western side of the village where I found an emaciated man whose wrinkled face defied his age. He had all the signs of man who had had terrible days of torment; nevertheless, I endured the ritual which took almost two hours. When the so-called 'great man' finished and told me that I was free to go, I became very angry because I realised that I had been cheated. I had lost a lot of money towards bus fare and fee to the spirit medium for his worthless services, yet the pain remained.

I left for home wondering whether I could ever be healed. I was angry against my ancestor whom I felt had let me down, yet I had performed all the rituals they needed to appease them. I also wondered whether there was a god somewhere and if he was, why he was so discriminatory. I had seen some people prospering, yet it seemed they never bothered to follow our African traditional way of worship. They only went to church and never honoured and respected their ancestral spirits.

In African traditional religion, one is never correct. After every ritual, one goes to another spirit medium to verify if the ancestors had accepted the prayer. It is always said there was something that was not done well. So when I went to other spirit mediums in Chiredzi, some 700 km south of Harare, they told me that the rituals had not been correctly done. I then went through some more rituals paying lots of money to the spirit mediums and some for buying goats including white chickens and black chickens, but it all failed.

I then turned to 'man of god' of the apostolic churches. That is when I discovered that they operate as a branch of the spirit mediums who operate under the organization called:

Zimbabwe National African Traditional Healer's Association (ZINATHA). These so-called 'prophets' also called 'Faith Healers' are operating under licence of ZINATHA.

I wondered how they could be used of God if they are licensed by an organization that stands for devil worship. However, I tried them and they failed to heal me.

I lost all hope. I did not know that I had the key to my healing which is my will and choice to turn to one true God, the Creator of universe who revealed Himself through His Son Jesus Christ. I still had one card left. So I joined several of the main line churches to no avail.

It was after I had given up hope that my sister-in-law invited me to their church. I got there and the pastor who preached that day preached from Exodus 3: 1-6. When he said, 'Take off the sandals that you were using going to n'angas and false prophets for the place you are in is holy. Jesus loves you. He died for you and wants to heal you. Turn to Jesus,' I was touched so much that when he made an altar call, I went to the front with tears running down my cheeks. When he laid hands on me and prayed for me, I felt as if a bucket full of ice-cold water had been poured over me. Then I felt warm; within a matter of seconds, the headache and stomach pain had stopped. This was twenty five years ago. I have never had those pains again since that day. I give glory to my Lord and Saviour Jesus Christ who called me and accepted me as I was and delivered me from my misery. If you have any type of problems, try Jesus Christ, give him a chance. Why die of it when Jesus died for it?

Chapter 7

Devil is Not against Worship of God

The devil is not against people who believe in God for he knows it is a belief natural to man. The devil fights with all that he has against the name Jesus Christ and belief in him. God has decreed that whosoever wants to come to him must do so through Jesus Christ who is the express image of Him (Col. 1: 15)

Before I went into full-time ministry, I led a team that went about preaching and disciplining people. I noted during those days that if you approached people in the name of God, you would be accepted and they could easily join you in your singing. But when I said, 'Jesus loves you' and that no one comes to the Father but by Him, I used to face resistance, anger, and verbal attack. I then asked why? I found out that it is because Jesus is the personification of all that God wanted to say to mankind. He is the answer to mankind's cry under the devil's oppression. The devil does not want people to know Jesus as he is because he knows the power in the name of Jesus. God has put all His power in this name. The blood that was shed on the cross paid the full price.

There are some who are deceived by the devil to believe that they want to pray direct to Jehovah God and refuse to go through Jesus Christ. They call him a little god and that he was created and is the firstborn to all creation. If you reject Jesus as Saviour, you cannot reach God.

> 'No one who denies the Son has the father; Whoever acknowledges the Son has the father also.' (1 John 2: 23, NIV)

> 'He who has the Son has life; he who does not have the Son of God does not have Life.' (1 John 5: 12, NIV)

I have noted that some people trust books written by people who have a belief of their own about the Bible. These people don't believe what the Bible says. It's surprising to see that people trust strangers but don't trust their God. People are prepared to board a bus or any vehicle without asking if the driver has license. They can even sleep whilst the vehicle travels on because they are confident to arrive safely. When God says, 'Trust me, I know the plans I have for you to prosper you and not to harm you' in Jeremiah 29: 11, people doubt.

Therefore, the devil thrives in man's doubt at their peril. Lack of faith kills as happened to Jews in wilderness though they had been delivered and seen many signs and wonders. God destroyed those who did not believe or I should say in my own thinking those who held on to their evil past and desired the familiar without God instead of the unknown with God as Abraham did (Jude 5 and Gen. 12: 1-9).

The problem I see in people who believe Jesus is a created being and that He is not God and therefore they decide to pray directly to Jehovah is their interpretation of John 1: 1 which says,

'In the beginning was the Word, and the Word was with God, and the Word was God.'

In the Greek original, there is no definite article 'the' in the last part of this verse which means we cannot translate it 'and the word was the God'. Thus to Jehovah witnesses, they translate as 'And the Word was a god', but this cannot be justified. The word 'the' may not be reflected in the Greek, but neither is the word 'A' even they put it to make it sound better. It even sounds much better if translated as it is in Greek. The grammatical construction without the definite article simply means that:

The word was of the essence of god or simply, *the word was god*

No 'the' and no 'A'.

You can see from my earlier statement that 95 per cent truth plus 5 per cent lies comes out to be all lies. Just the letter 'A' in sentence with forty-one letters changed the meaning to even justify the spelling of God to be done in a small 'g' as 'god' because the all powerful all knowing, almighty God cannot be called 'A' but 'THE' or just God who is the only one who is infinite. This effort in interpretation is so important that if it's believed, it determines your destination.

Imagine an aeroplane taking off from London to USA. But being one degree of course, by the time it reaches USA, it will probably be over 100 miles off course and lost. If you believe and accept this interpretation of John 1: 1 in the meaning Jesus is 'a god', you will be over 100 miles from salvation; whether you are active in your church or even if you are the pastor or leader or archbishop or whatever title you may give yourself, you are not of His and you are heading for Hell unless you repent.

He only baptises those who accept Him as Lord and Saviour who was 100 per cent human and 100 per cent divine.

> 'Now if any man have not the spirit of Christ, He is none of his.'
> (Rom. 8: 9, KJV)

Jesus once said to the Jews, 'If you don't believe me believe on account of the miracles I perform.' You should also likewise believe Him when He says He is God. Has your church or belief been able to transform you? If not, quickly get out of it and seek a church that preaches, believes, and uplifts Jesus as Lord and Saviour. If you accept Him as such, your transformation will follow and you will know when you are saved and free from bondage.

You may be afraid to move, but I want you to know that fear is a force that the devil uses to keep people under his control; in other words, we can say fear is belief in Devil. It has power. Faith is a belief in God and is also a force which the devil cannot stand against. If you act on fear, you have given devil legal right to make it come to pass.

> 'For the thing which I greatly feared is come upon me, and that which I was afraid of is come unto me.' (Job 3: 25)

Devil gives you fear, then gives you worry, and then it develops into depression which it is said by medical experts destroys immune system. Immune system is our defence against foreign bodies that may cause diseases. Now if it's destroyed, no wonder medical bills accumulate. Why don't you give your life to Jesus who will keep it for you?

CHAPTER 8

Great Deception

Jesus's disciples went to ask him for a sign of his coming.

> 'Tell us. When shall these things be? And what shall be the sign of thy coming and of the end of the world? And Jesus answered and said unto them, take heed that no man deceive you. For many shall come in my name saying I am Christ; And shall deceive many' (Matt. 24: 3-0 5, KJV)

There are two meanings to this. The obvious meaning which is quickly seen is those who come saying 'I am Christ'; these we have seen and we have heard off. Though many are still being deceived by them, they are not as deceptive and dangerous as the next group. The other meaning which is deeper and more deceiving is they 'shall come in my name'. They come in place of Christ. They don't come against Christ. The first group those who read the Bible can easily discard away as phoney, but this second group, they go to Bible Colleges, graduate, and come out saying, 'Praise God, in the name of Jesus'. Everything they do seem to be for Jesus, yet if you look at the fruit thereof.

> 'Thus by their fruit you will recognize them.' (Matt. 7: 20)

These come in sheep's clothing, yet they are wolves. They are false prophets. Remember Jesus's warning.

'Not everyone who says to me, "Lord Lord," will enter the kingdom of heaven, but only he who does the will of my father who is in heaven'. (Matt. 7: 21)

They come for money, prestige, power, and benefits that go with the ministry. They use any means to get to the top, yet they have nothing to do with God and His son Jesus Christ. The name of Jesus is only a means to glory. They have no character; that is why, among the charismatic movement, we find in leadership homosexuals, lesbians, adulterers, and all sorts of criminals.

One may ask what is the will of God as the disciples of Jesus did. They thought the will of God is to do works that are acceptable to God, so they went to find out from Jesus.

'Then they asked, what must we do to do the works God requires?' Jesus answered, 'The work of God is this: to believe in the One He has sent.' (John 6: 28-29, NIV)

Who did God sent who should be believed?

'But when the time had full come, God sent his Son, born of a woman, born under the law, to redeem those under the law, that we might receive the full rights of sons.' (Gal. 4: 4, NIV)

Therefore, to do the will of God is to believe in Jesus Christ the son of God who came to redeem us. If then the will of God is for us to believe in Jesus Christ, where does Mary the mother of Jesus come in? I have searched the Bible to see if there is anywhere it is said Mary can plead on our behalf to Jesus for forgiveness but I found none. Also salvation comes when one hears the word of God and believes and accepts Jesus as Lord and Saviour.

No one can plead either through Mary or directly to God on behalf of a dead relative or friend to be forgiven and go to Heaven. To do so is to nullify the work done by Jesus on the cross. It means people are able to go to Heaven through their own effort. In short, Jesus died for nothing. Without demeaning Mary the mother of Jesus and the work she did, we just have to know that we can appreciate but never worship her. Only God is to be worshiped and Mary is not God. Scriptures tell us there is only one mediator not two.

'For there is one God and one mediator between God and men, the man Jesus Christ.' (1 Tim. 2: 5)

Some say Mary is the mother of God, yet we know God has no beginning, no father, and no mother. Jesus was conceived of the Holy Spirit in Mary's womb because it was the means by which he could come to the world and be accepted among people. If he had come in his glory, no one would stand and look at him. God is Spirit and we are mortal beings.

His problem to communicate with us would best be expressed as *Hal Lindsey* says in his book, *The Liberation of Planet Earth*. He gives an example of a naturalist who spent hours and days observing an anthill and watched the intricate manoeuvring of ants and developed a special affinity for them. One day, the naturalist saw a huge bulldozer in the distance and immediately realised that this anthill lay right in the path of the construction of a new road. The man panicked. He desperately searched his mind for a way to remove the ants. He scooped up handfuls of them, but they only bit him. He thought of building a fence around the ant pile, but realised the bulldozer would only tear it down. In his frenzied mind, he thought to himself, 'If only I could speak to them and tell them about the danger ahead of them. If only I could make them see that I am their friend and only want to save them from destruction.' But despite his great concern, he could think of how to communicate to them in a way they would understand. To be able to do that, he would have to become an ant himself, and yet retain the nature of a man so he could continue to clearly assess the problems and make it known to the ants.

This is exactly what Jesus did. He voluntarily put aside some of His attributes of deity and changed to be like us but retained his divine nature to be able to clearly see the danger we were facing and then with love direct us to Himself to be delivered from deaths.

Chapter 9

Why I Believe the Bible

I had lost hope, wanted to die, but I was full of fear of where I was going to go when I die. The pain I suffered was so unbearable and excruciating that I thought to die was better, especially because in our African custom, it is generally believed to die is to rest because in African context there is no judgment after death. I had lost a lot of money to false prophets, to witch doctors, to medical doctors, and in travelling. I almost lost my job which gave me money to pay these people because I could not perform to expected standards because of pain. I hated life, was withdrawn till I had no friends. My family especially my wife suffered so much, and I thank God and will praise my Lord Jesus Christ forever and ever for what He did. My wife could cook special meals, but I could not eat because of continuous stomach pains. I became so thin that if it were these days, I could have been put aside as one with the dreaded AIDS disease.

I did not want to talk because of severe headaches, and when I came back from work and my wife tried to cheer me up, she only received rude remarks.

After all this, imagine just sitting in the church and the gospel of Jesus Christ being preached. Then after an altar call or a call to repentance was made, I went up to receive my dear Lord who had been so faithful to keep me alive even when I was deep in sin and received new life and healing just because I believed.

I now understand why God says in Isaiah 1: 18, 'Come now, let us reason together'.

I believed the Bible and I got new life. I have so far seen many people healed of all sorts of diseases when I prayed for them as the Bible says in Mark 16: 17-18.

I believe the Bible because it is inspired of God.

'All scripture is given by inspiration of God' (2 Tim. 3: 16)

The Bible contains the mind of God, the state of man, the way of salvation, the doom of sinners, and the happiness of believers according to *The Gideon's International Bible* preface.'

Josh Macdowell in his book, *Evidence that demands a verdict*, Volume 1, spends time showing the uniqueness of the Bible as follows:

1. It is written over a 1 500 span

2. Written over 40 generations

3. Written by over 40 authors from every walk of life including kings, peasants, philosophers, fishermen, poets, statesmen, scholars etc. e.g. Solomon was a king, Amos was a herdsman, Moses—political leader, Peter—fishermen, Joshua—military general, Luke—doctor etc.

4. It was written in different places, Moses in wilderness, Jeremiah in dungeon, Daniel in hillside and in Palace, Paul inside prison walls, Luke while travelling, John on the isle of Patmos etc.

5. It was written in different times, David in times of War and Solomon in time of peace.

6. It was written in three continents Asia, Africa and Europe

It is the most hated and most wanted and loved book. Those who hated it tried to destroy it; some burned it, but the more it was burnt, the more it was spread. This wonderful book seems to thrive and grow in strength where there is opposition. It has been read by more people and published in more languages than any other book. Josh Macdowell quoting Hy Pickering says that about thirty 30 years ago, for the British and Foreign Bible Society to meet its demand, it had to publish, 'one copy every three seconds day and night, 22 copies every minute day and night, 1 369 copies every hour day and night; 32 876 copies every day in the year.' But this information was first published in 1981 followed by other reprints. So we may say this information is twenty years out of date so what about now?

In AD 303, Emperor Diocletian of Rome issued an edict to stop Christians from worshipping and to destroy their scriptures. The imperial letter was everywhere promulgated ordering the razing of the churches to the ground and destruction of the scriptures by fire. Surprisingly enough, twenty-five years later, Emperor Constantine issued also an edict to give freedom of worship throughout the Empire with special favours to Christianity and ordered fifty copies of the Bible to be prepared at government expense.

Bernard Ramm states: 'A thousand times over, the death knell of the bible has been sounded, the funeral precession formed, the inscription cut on the tombstone, and the committal read. But somehow the corpse never stays put. No other book has been so chopped, knifed, sifted, scrutinized and vilified . . . has been subject to such a mass attach as the Bible. With such venom and skepticism, with such thoroughness and erudition. Upon every chapter, line and tenet.'

'The Bible is still loved by millions, read by millions, and studied by millions'. In this book whose grand subject is Jesus Christ of Nazareth we are told of this man who without arms of war and money conquered more millions than Alexander the great, Caesar, Mohammed, and Napoleon. He without going to school and learning the basics of medicine has healed more millions of people than all the medical doctors put together. A man who was rejected by His own but loved and cared so much as to die for His persecutors and all people on earth and those to be born so that through faith in Him they may have eternal life.

Many people are deceived by the devil because they do not read the Bible as a result they are swept by every wind of doctrine that comes. Those who lead people astray discourage people from reading the Bible but as I have already said the most dangerous deceptive method of the devil is that of not coming against Christ but coming for or in place of Christ. Therefore, some encourage the reading of scriptures and also use scriptures to preach from, but they deceive their followers by telling them that they have new revelation direct from God.

We must note here that God will not say and do anything that contradicts his written word.

> 'For I am the Lord, I charge not; therefore ye sons of Jacob are not consumed'
>
> (Mal. 3: 6)

There is serious eternal danger to those who add to what the Bible says and those who subtract. When you come across such people, get out, it's the devil speaking. God operates in accordance to His word which He spoke through His son Jesus Christ.

> If any man shall add unto these things, God shall add unto Him the plagues that are written in this book: and if any man Take away from the words of the book of this prophecy, God shall Take away his part out of the book of life (Rev. 22: 18-19, KJV)

There you are if you love popularity, riches, and human respect so much that you use God's word to get these worldly things.

I am concerned about those who are cheated. God has made the word available and simple to understand. Some are being taught that once you are saved you are forever saved even if you go back to the evil you used to do.

May I ask you? If you get a driver's license but you decide to drive anyway you want recklessly, without due care and attention, dangerous to other road users, drunken, etc. will your government not revoke the license? Will they say once you get your driver's license you are forever going to drive legally? You have to abide by the rules of the road as stated by the government. Failure to do so would mean license will be withdrawn. But the withdrawal of license does not stop you from driving illegally. It does not make you unable to drive. You can still drive, but it will be illegal. The same with the way of salvation. You must live by the rules of the word of God if you want to remain saved. Allow the Holy Spirit to work in you and transform you. If you backslide, you can still preach if you want, you can carry your Bible around and be a member of church, but it does not make you regain your Heavenly Citizenship. You must repent and confess your sins and turn to God to be accepted. He only needs a contrite heart.

CHAPTER 10

The Finished Work of the Cross

Man, because of his pride, does not want to accept something given free. I have seen marriages that have broken down because of the husband's pride. The husband does not work, but the wife has either money from her father's deceased estate or the father has businesses and offers to employ his son-in-law who with anger rejects the offer. The wife is beaten from trying to help supply the family needs. The husband keeps on saying, 'I am able to look after my family,' but he is not able to buy even a loaf of bread.

Eventually the wife decides to leave, but the husband who is blinded by pride does not even see what wrong he is doing. He keeps on blaming the wife throughout the divorce process.

This pride cause man to refuse to accept that Jesus Christ finished all that was needed to redeem man and make him reconciled to God. Man wants to do something to be accepted by God. He wants to have the blood of Jesus plus his own works. This only gives him more pride because his salvation is based on how much he has done to help Jesus Christ to complete his redemption. Note here that man's religions are ministries of 'do and don't', but God's way of salvation is 'done'. You don't have to do except to believe. Jesus made us worthy to be used of Him, to be His children, and to be the righteousness of God through Him.

People love the Law of Moses because it gave man self-glory on the basis of being better than others and being more acceptable to God than others. They did not know that they all came short of the glory of God. Law was not meant to accord righteousness but to reveal sin that was in man. It was to show them their inability to fulfil its demands so that they can turn to the Saviour, Messiah Jesus Christ.

If you put crabs in a basket, they will not come out, not because they can't but because they are selfish and proud. It does not help for one crab to be on top of all the others but still being in basket because if food is outside the basket, it will still starve as those at the bottom. They pull each other down because each one wants to be on top. The same with humans who want to be saved by their own works. God's righteousness is so high that it cannot be reached by man even if we add all the righteousness of all people on earth. We will still come short of His glory. We climb on each other, blame each other, and pride in being better and more holy than others not knowing that such thinking is proof of failure to attain God's Holiness.

It's proof of pride and selfishness. It's proof of failure to keep the law which is one reason why the law came to show us our inability to keep it and point us to one who would be able to keep the law on our behalf so that when we believe in Him, we will be accepted as having been able to keep the law.

Righteousness of God

Abraham discovered that being made right with God had nothing to do with his good deeds which would make him acceptable to God rather than boast in his deeds; the scripture says, 'Abraham believed God, and God counted him righteous because of his faith.' (Rom. 4: 3)

Abraham was counted righteous many years before he was circumcised which means he was accepted not because of circumcision but because he believed.

'Circumcision was a sign that Abraham already had faith and that God had already accepted him and declared him to be righteous—even before he was circumcised. So Abraham is the spiritual father of those who have faith but have not been circumcised. They are counted as righteous because of their faith.' (Rom. 4: 11)

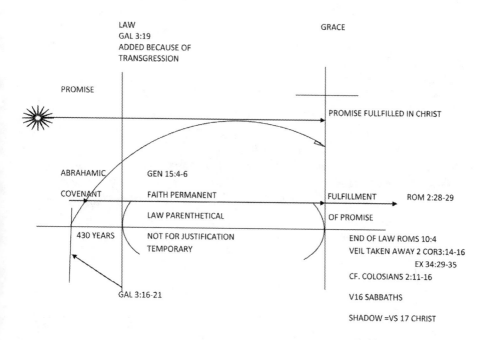

God's way of salvation has always been by grace through faith.

> 'For when god made promise to Abraham, because he could swear by no greater, he swear by himself, saying, surely blessing I will bless thee, and multiplying I will multiply thee. And so, after he had patiently endured, he obtained the promise.' (Heb. 6: 13-15)

> 'For the promise, that he should be the heir of the world, was not to Abraham, or to his seed, through the law, but through the righteousness of faith, for if they which are of the law be heirs, faith is made void, and the promise made of none effect.' (Romans 4: 13-14)

The promise to Abraham was made 430 years before the law and the promise is fulfilled in Christ Jesus who came Himself to be the son of Abraham. He fulfilled also the Davidic covenant, 'Your throne shall be established forever.' (2 Sam. 7: 16). For no human being even David would live forever, the promise could only make sense if it's directed to Jesus Christ. Isaac as a picture came as son of promise to prefigure Christ who would fulfil all the promise.

The law came for a different purpose. It was not to accord righteousness but to reveal sin and that man was not able to meet and attain the God kind of righteousness which only God himself through His son Jesus could accord. The law is a later parenthetical statement, which does not nullify a covenant previously given. Nb. A statement in brackets does not state a new idea or replace former statement but clarifies the former statement.

For example, 'Christ has redeemed us from the curse of the law, having become a curse for us (for it is written,' cursed is everyone who hangs on a tree').

The bracketed statement is only clarifying the former statement. This is what the law is like, it did not come to replace faith but rather to reveal to us that the way to God is by grace through faith. We cannot attain it on our own effort just as it was impossible to keep the law and attain salvation. Law was one not 613 ordinances, to reach God one had to keep all of it, break one and you have broken all. Salvation has always been by grace through faith.

For Christ is the end of the law for righteousness to everyone who believes. (Rom. 10: 4)

Not that we do not observe the law but that our keeping and upholding the law is because we are children of God whose nature is no longer that of sin but righteousness. We are no longer slaves to sin. We are saved and brought into the kingdom of God to do the good works created for us and not to keep the law that we might be saved but that we are saved therefore we abide by the law as children.

For he is not a Jew who is one outwardly, nor is circumcision that which is outward in the flesh; but he is a Jew who is one inwardly; and circumcision is that of the heart, in the spirit, not in the letter; whose praise is not from men but from god. (Rom. 2: 28-29)

In whom also ye are circumcised with the circumcision made without hands, in putting off the body of the sins of the flesh, by the circumcision of Christ; buried with him in baptism wherein also ye are risen with him through the faith of the operation of God, who has raised him from the dead. And you, being dead in your sins and the uncircumcision of your flesh hath he quickened together with him, having forgiven you all trespasses. (Col. 2: 11-13)

Let no man therefore judge you in meat, or in drink, or in respect of an holyday, or of the new moon, or of the Sabbath days. (Col. 2: 16)

In all this we are not rejecting the Law. Law is not contrary to the promise; rather the two are complementary. The Law demanded righteousness but was powerless to provide it. Its function was to prepare for the gospel by making people conscious of their sin and their need for a saviour.

When men fell, God did not speak forth his salvation but He had to come himself into the scene in the person of Jesus Christ.

'Who is the image of the invisible God.' (Col. 1: 15)

Some people reject Jesus Christ and spend time in searching the scriptures for eternal life, yet every time they look at the scripture, the scriptures direct them to Jesus.

'Search the scriptures, for in them ye think ye have eternal life: and they are they which testify of me and ye will not come to me that ye might have life.' (John 5: 39-40, KJV)

Also see NIV,

'You diligently study the scriptures because you think that by them you possess eternal life. These are the scriptures that testify about me. Yet you refuse to come to me to have life.' (John 5: 39-40)

When man fell, God instituted man's reconciliation to him as early as in Genesis 3: 15. The whole Bible is a story of God and His people restoring them till we get to Galatians 4: 4 when Jesus Christ the son of God arrived born of a woman under the law to save those under the law. It only needed God to deliver His people. The blood of animals only covered but did not take away sin. God is holy and cannot look upon sin. Jesus came to take away sin (John 1: 29).

If God looks at one with sin, He destroys him. But when He sees blood of an innocent victim, He is appeased and His wrath is withdrawn. He has said without the shedding of blood, there is no forgiveness of sin. Our own works are not blood, therefore to try and be accepted of God on the basis of works means one has failed before he has even started.

Jesus came to be like us so that we would accept Him and also that He could have blood to be shed for remission of sin. The devil had to be defeated by a human being not by God, that is why Jesus, 'the Word that was with God, the Word that was God,' had to become man that in Him and Through Him as a human being, humanity mighty be set free from the power of the devil.

Forgiveness of sin can only be through the shedding of blood of an innocent victim. God is spirit, therefore Jesus as God would not defeat the devil on our behalf in His capacity as God who is spirit. He had to have a body with blood to be shed as a human being.

> 'Wherefore when He cometh into the world, He saith, Sacrifice
> and Offering thou Wouldest not, but a body hast thou prepared for
> me;' (Heb.10:5 KJV)

Only His blood could do the job because it had to be blood of one without sin. All men sinned and their blood was contaminated by sin therefore unacceptable to redeem man. All men were thus disqualified. Jesus was born of a virgin but was conceived of the Holy Spirit and not of human father. His blood had no sin by virtue of his supernatural way of conception.

'For he hath made him to be sin for us, who knew no sin, that we might be made the righteousness of God in him.' (2 Cor. 5: 51, KJV)

If you believe in Jesus, His righteousness is credited to your account and God declares you justified on the basis of Him who paid the full price or penalty of sin which is death. When you go to court especially to Supreme Court, you need an advocate who will argue your case as though he committed the crime himself. You will be seated and quiet. Jesus had been qualified to be our advocate as he was 100 per cent human and 100 per cent divine. He lived as human beings but overcame being sinless.

> 'For we have not an high priest which cannot be touched with the
> feeling of our Infirmities; but was in all points tempted like as we
> are, yet without sin.' (Heb.4:15,KJV)

> 'For there is one God, and one mediator between God and men,
> The man Jesus Christ: who gave himself a ransom for all.' (1 Tim.
> 2: 5, KJV)

This scripture nullifies anyone who claims to lead people to God, or any religion that has its own means, ways and methods of reaching God After all if there were other acceptable means of reaching God, Jesus would not have come to suffer rejection, pain, abuse, torture, and death for only a few people who would want to accept His way to God as another of the many ways.

No one can bribe His way to heaven; it's either through Jesus Christ the way and wisdom of God or never.

'Christ the Power of God, and the wisdom of God.' (1 Cor. 1: 24, KJV)

'I am the way, the truth, and the life: no man cameth unto the father but by me.' (John 14: 6, KJV)

Believe this to be wise and safe; if you do not, this may be your last chance for salvation because you do not know when you will be called from this earth into eternity. If you enter eternity without Jesus, you are heading for eternal torment. If you believe you can get to heaven by any means other than Jesus Christ whether its works or your own religion, you must know that the devil has injected you with his 'lethal dose'. Some may say why do you have to be so absolute and dogmatic that Jesus is the only way?

It is because truth defends itself, take time to read the Holy Bible with an open mind and you will see why we say that. Only Jesus fulfilled all that was said about him by the Old Testament prophets. Only He rose from the dead, and we have an empty tomb as eternal testimony to the fact that He is alive.

Debt of Sin

In the book by Hal Lindsey entitled, *The Liberation of Planet Earth*, he gives a very concise explanation of what used to happen during the great dominion of Rome. He states that it was assured by Caesar that every Roman citizen owed him perfect allegiance and obedience to his laws. Justice was swift to be enforced. If a man were found guilty of breaking the law and sentenced to prison, an itemised list was made of each infraction and its corresponding penalty. This list was, in essence, a record of law the man had failed to live up to, the laws of Caesar. It was called a 'Certificate of Debt'

When the man was taken to his prison cell, this certificate of debt was nailed to his cell door so that anyone passing by could tell that the man had been justly condemned. They could also see limitations of his punishment. People could also see that if a prisoner was kept in prison more than the appropriate penalty, it was illegal.

When the man had served his time and was released, he would be handed the yellowed tattered certificate of debt with the words 'Paid in Full' written across it. He could never again be imprisoned for those crimes as long as he could produce his cancelled certificate of debt.

But before the sentence was paid, that certificate of debt stood between him and freedom. It continued to witness to the fact that the imprisoned man had failed to live accordingly to the laws of Rome and was, in essence, an offense to Caesar. Man owes God perfect obedience to His Holy laws as summarised in the Ten Commandments and the Sermon on the Mount. Man failed to live by the standards set by God and has became an offense to the very character of God, and the eternal court of justice has pronounced the death sentence upon man.

'For the wages of sin is death: but the gift of God is eternal life through Jesus Christ our Lord.' (Rom. 6: 23)

Hall goes on to say a certificate of debt was prepared against every person who would ever live listing his failure to live in thought, word, and deed in accordance with the law of God. This death sentence has become a *Debt of Sin* which has to be paid, either by man or, if possible, someone qualified to take his place.

Paul puts it powerfully to convince his hearers that they had been set free from their sinful indebtedness to God.

> 'When you were dead in your sins and in the uncircumcision of your sinful nature, God made you alive with Christ. He forgave us all our sins, having cancelled the written code, with its regulations, that was against us and that stood opposed to us; he took it away, nailing it to the cross. And having disarmed the powers and authorities, he made a public spectacle of them, triumphing over them by the cross.' (Col. 2: 13-15, NIV)

The laws of God only became a problem because we can't keep them. Paul gives us a fantastic picture of Jesus taking my certificate and your certificate of debt and nailing them to the cross. In doing this, it was tantamount to saying He was guilty of every sin listed on every certificate of every man who would ever be born. He did not only volunteered to take our certificates of debt but also their penalty which was death. I like Hal Lindsey's Greek interpretation of Jesus's last words on the cross. Our Lord's victorious cry was exactly what the Roman judge would write across a released criminals' Certificate of Debt to show that all his penalty had been paid and was free at last. The words are in John 19: 30 'It is finished' translated.

Tetelestai! Paid in Full

Thank you, Lord Jesus the Prince of Peace, you gave us peace with God.

> 'Therefore, being justified by faith, we have peace with God through our Lord Jesus Christ.' (Rom. 5: 1, KJV)

All my sins are paid for, past, present, and future. Glory to His name I shall forever praise His Holy Name.

My Saviour persevered in humiliation, pain, and rejection for my sake. Now even the devil, his demons, and hell can shout its fury against me, but I am not frightened. I am secure in His hands that were pierced because of my sins. My friend, why do you want to suffer yet Jesus suffered for you? He is calling you to take salvation free; yours is only to believe in Him and invite him in your life. If you have not surrendered your life to him, it is your time.

Dear friend, join me to Heaven through our Lord Jesus. He will not fail you.

If you want assurance of eternal life, please pray this prayer. Be serious, it's a matter of life and death.

Sinner's Prayer

Lord Jesus, I want to thank you for dying for me. I now know that all my sins were paid for. I am a sinner and need your forgiveness. Lord, forgive me all my transgressions against you. Cleanse me from all unrighteousness. Fill me up with your Spirit and write my name in your book of life. Lord, I renounce all my evil ways and accept you as my Lord and Saviour. Take this life Lord and use it. In your name I pray. Amen.

If you have done this with all your heart, you are saved. Thank God you are a child of God. Now seek a Bible-believing church where they believe in Jesus as God and as Lord and Saviour who came on earth in flesh to save sinners. Buy a Bible and read it daily. That is your Spiritual food, and you need it to grow. Making a sinner's prayer, inviting Lord Jesus into your heart, and confessing and renouncing your sins is the way to be born-again. Your spirit which was dormant and insensitive to God will be regenerated to desire, love, and crave for the word of God and pray. You are not saved when you are baptised but when you believe in Jesus Christ. Baptism is a public demonstration of an inward transformation which took place when you believed in Jesus Christ.

> 'But as many as received him, to them He gave the power to become the sons of God, even to them that believe on his name.' (John 1: 12, KJV)

If you believe you are born-again of the Spirit and the Power referred to here is the authority to be called children of God. All other religions of the world related to God just as God but Christianity accords us a special position of being children. We can call God our father just as Jesus because we are adopted into God's kingdom through Jesus. We now have a relationship with the living God so we fellowship and have communion with him.

You are aware that one cannot belong to UTETE family unless he or she is biologically born of UTETE parents. It is the same with salvation, for one to be a child of God, he or she must be born of the spirit of God through faith in Christ. Don't be fooled by the devil that because of what you did, you are unacceptable. Jesus came for the very people like you. He came to seek and save that which was lost. One time he even said that it was the sick that seek the doctor. You are sick in your spirit if you have not accepted Christ as your personal Saviour. Call him in to heal you and cleanse you.

'Therefore, there is now no condemnation for those who are in Christ Jesus because through Christ Jesus the law of the spirit of Life set me free from the law of sin and death.' (Rom. 8: 1-2, NIV)

God does not condemn you for what you did because that is what Jesus came for and died for. You will be judged for refusing a free gift of God, the finished work of redemption done by Jesus for us. The question will not be 'why did you steal?' but, 'what did you do with Jesus who was preached to you?' Before he came we were condemned, held under bondage of sin, but thank God, Jesus came and broke the chains of bondage and restored the relationship that was severed because of sin. You probably hate yourself so much that you cannot forgive yourself as a result you are running away from friends, relatives, and God who loves. You probably were abused and the devil reminds you and tells you it was your fault. He is a liar. It was his fault, but he is cunning and will not accept responsibility. He accuses you for what he did.

'The devil wants you to be bitter against God for what he, the devil has done. He knows once you are angry against God you will never be saved and set free.'

But you can overcome him through Christ.

'They overcame him by the blood of the lamb and by the word of their testimony.' (Rev. 12: 11, NIV)

If you have accepted Christ as Saviour, testify to the devil of the great work that Christ did on the cross and that you are set free by His blood. If he reminds you of your past, remind him of his past, 'how foolish and damn he had been to be kicked out of heaven' to put it as Joel Osteen does. Also remind him of his future in lake of fire. When Jesus cried his cry of victory 'Tetelestai' 'It is finished' 'Paid in Full', the veil that separated the Holy place from the Holy of Holies was rent top to bottom. The Holy place was entered once a year by the High Priest alone with blood which he offered for himself and for the sins of all the people.

The veil was rent into two top to bottom to show that salvation came from above down to people and it was not of man and that man had no part in its delivery. It was rent to reveal the Holy places so that it became open for all not for the High Priest only. The veil symbolised the body of Christ which was broken for our sins. When he died, his death revealed the glory of God which was hidden behind His flesh and forever opened the way to God.

'By new and living way, which he hath consecrated for us, through the veil, that is to say, his flesh' (Heb. 10: 20, KJV)

His body was torn as he paid our debt of sin so that whosoever believes in him will not perish but have everlasting life. His entry into Holy Place was not to be repeated. His payment was sufficient once and for all.

No other addition is needed even our works. Works should only be as a result of our love for Him and should naturally flow from within the heart that has been transformed and then manifest good works as the evidence of the work done inwardly.

'He did not enter by means of the blood of goats and calves; but he entered the most Holy place once for all by his own blood, having obtained eternal redemption.' (Heb. 9: 12, NIV)

Heaven is open to everybody through Jesus Christ. You no longer need a priest, bishop, archbishop, or whatever title you give him to pray for you to receive forgiveness of sins. You can pray at any time at any place to God through Jesus Christ and you will be accepted. Your salvation is based on agreeing with God that you are a sinner and unable to help yourself and need a Saviour. Agree with God that Jesus Christ is the answer and believe in the finished work of the cross. Not agreeing with God in these areas means you are making him a liar. My friend, hell is real and sure just as you know the sun rises daily; whether it is cloudy or not, it comes up. Soon and very soon that sun will rise marking your last day on this world.

Are you sure you are ready to face the awesome Creator of the universe? Have you done enough good works for him to say, 'By virtue of your good works come into Heaven'? Do not be fooled, you cannot determine entry qualifications to Heaven because you do not have the authority.

You know that you cannot go to a foreign country without a passport and demand to be allowed entry because in your country it is known you are a good citizen. You only get entry on the basis of that country's entry qualifications, which may be unacceptable to you, but if you want to enter that country, you just have to comply or return to your country.

God, the supreme ruler of the universe, has determined, directed, and sealed His entry requirements to Heaven eternally. The passport and VISA for Heaven is Jesus Christ and His blood. If you have backslidden, you have an expired passport. You need to renew it before your departure date or else entry will be denied.

Remember, it's like all humanity is on a huge bus, those who are being born are boarding the bus of life. Those who die are reaching their destination and getting out.

It does not matter how much friendship you have built in the bus, it does not make your friend or you change destination. Each one is going to his home regardless of the state of the home. God prepared your entry into this world. It is now your duty to prepare your own exit. The bus of life is not a permanent home. As the wheels turn, seconds and minutes tick away, each one on board is getting closer to his own destination. Each one is going to his home regardless of the state of the home.

This world's judges can forgive only when they are satisfied you are not guilt. If you are guilt, they punish you. Our father in Heaven forgives those who are proven guilt. If you are guilty of any crime even if you are to be killed by this world's judge, if you accept Christ as your Lord and Saviour, you are forgiven and given eternal life.

This world is crazy. I have seen during my years as pastor of an assembly in a police camp and prison warder's camp that the law enforcement officers are themselves bound by the very same things they arrest others for. After work, one finds police officers smoking dagga, mbanje, and any intoxicating drugs. But among the prisoners, one would find former criminals who were saved and delivered from demonic control by the blood of Jesus Christ. The one bound was now looking after the delivered and free. I used to hear several police officers and prison warders after conversion testifying of the horrible things they used to do. The devil truly does not respect your uniform, position in society, financial status, and education. But he is afraid of the power of the blood of Jesus.

One may be a very good, honest government official, but it does not mean he is accepted by the heavenly kingdom because it's another government with its own rules. It is important to turn to Jesus Christ so that the good work can flow from a transformed sanctified heart. God's standard of righteousness is Jesus Christ. If anyone tries to go to God or attain righteousness by other means and ways, it is not accepted.

But if one believes in Jesus Christ, righteousness is credited to him with the result that God declares that person righteous and justified on the basis of one who was human but was able to live and fulfil the requirements of God. This person is Jesus Christ who though He was God, He humbled himself to be like man and died the most painful and humiliating death on the cross.

Having completed what He came for, 'God exalted him and gave him name above every name that every knee must bow of all things in Heaven and things in earth and things under earth to the name of Jesus and that every tongue should confess that Jesus Christ is Lord to the glory of God the Father.' (Phil. 2: 9-11)

No human being has lived or one living and will live in a manner acceptable to God. Accepting Jesus is therefore simply logical to believe in the one acceptable by God and not try to argue with God.

There are those who claim to heal the sick and save all sorts of problems and claim to foretell the future. These people claim to be used of God's spirit, but they never mention the name of Jesus in their prayers and even when one joins them. They claim to baptise people, but what they do is not done as it is stated in the Bible. Jesus is the one who baptises with the Holy Spirit; therefore, if one does not pray to God through Jesus for baptism of the Spirit, the devil gives his own. We can therefore conclude that it is the spirit of the devil they use.

Who Is God?

The one God is Triune (one God in three persons, not three gods). There are three distinct persons but of one essence or substance—the Father, Son, and Holy Spirit. Often the term 'God' designates the first person of the Trinity, God the Father, God is a spiritual being without a physical body. He is personal and involved with people. He created the universe out of nothing. He is eternal, changeless, holy, loving, and perfect. God is all powerful or omnipotent, omnipresent, present everywhere at the same time, omniscient knowing everything at the same time. He loved the world and sent his son Jesus Christ to redeem the sinners.

Who Is Jesus Christ?

Jesus is God the second person of the Trinity. As God the Son (not created firstborn of humanity), *He has always existed and was never created*. He is fully 100 per cent God and fully 100 per cent human (the two natures joined, but not mixed). As the second person of the Trinity, he is coequal with God the Father and God the Holy Spirit. In becoming man, He was begotten through the Holy Spirit and born of a virgin Mary. Jesus is the only *way* to the father, salvation, and eternal life. He died on the cross according to God's plan, as full sacrifice and payment for our sins. He rose from the dead on the third day, spiritually and physically immortal. For the next forty days, he was seen by more than 500 eyewitnesses. His wounds were touched, and he ate meals after resurrection. He physically accented to Heaven. Jesus will come again visibly and physically at the end of the world. Jesus is all that God wanted to say to humanity. He is the grand subject of the Holy Bible. He is the Saviour of the world and God.

'I, even am the Lord, and apart from me there is no savior.'
(Isa. 43: 11, NIV)

'For the Son of Man is come to seek and to save that which was lost.'
(Luke 19: 10, KJV)

God gave all power and authority to Jesus. Nowhere in the world have I heard of any person who was healed of any sickness, disease, or resurrected from the dead in the *name of God, Mary, or any other name*. God has given this power to Jesus who said,
'All power is given unto me in Heaven and in Earth.' (Matt. 28: 18)
The miracle that happened in 2004 in Harare, Zimbabwe, as reported below is proof that resurrection, healing, deliverance, etc, is only through Jesus Christ. We can only access this power if we focus and believe in the finished work done by Jesus on the Cross of Calvary, his resurrection, ascension to heaven, inheritance and his enthronement as King of Kings and Lord of Lords.
From left to right: Mrs Garawadya child's mother, Mrs Maria Utete, Myself, Blessmore, and Mr Garawadya.

Dead Child Resurrected from Death on 14 March 2004
Rev. Lukas Utete holding Blessmore Garawadya after resurrection.
*** *Article By Permission of the Parents* ***

It was on 14 March 2004 while Rev. Lukas Utete and Mrs Maria Utete were pastors at AFM Mt Pleasant Miracle Centre when God visited and miraculously resurrected Blessmore from the dead.

In the morning, as we were going to church, I told my wife that though I had prepared notes for Bible Study, I had a strong feeling that we were not going to have Bible study. We got to the church and started our usual praise and worship till it was 9.30 a.m. when I stood, took my Bible and notes, and started to go to the pulpit. Just as I arrived and put my Bible on the podium, I had commotion and saw people rushing some to the back and some towards the pulpit.

Before I could tell what was happening, I saw a number of people coming towards me with an infant I thought was asleep. The mother was crying and lifted the child to me. It was then that I heard that something had happened to the child as a result he had stopped breathing. I got the child in my hands and started to pray. I told the whole church to pray. We all went into prayer. I felt the child getting cold the whole of his body. *The child was truly not breathing.* I put him close to my chest as I prayed walking up and down the church. After some time, I opened my eyes and looked at the child.

Suddenly a vision I had had while I was at Living Waters Bible College in 1997 flashed before me. In that vision, we had gone for evangelism with the then Overseer M. Shumbambiri who was teaching us the book of Acts then. At the crusade, a child died and Overseer Shumbambiri told us to pray for the dead child as part of the training. I took the child, lifted him, prayed, and he came back to life.

When the vision flashed, I saw that the face of the child we were praying for was the exact face I had seen in the vision some seven years before. I became excited and my faith exploded so much that I held the child in the air, shook him, and shouted, 'Wake up in *Jesus's name.*' Immediately, I felt assured that the child was back. *It was exactly 10.15 a.m. which means the boy had been cold and not breathing for forty-five minutes.*

I called the mother and gave her the child who was now breathing but was asleep. Some elders' wives (names not given because permission had not been sort as some are out of the country) decided to take the child to Avenues Clinic. They rushed to the car while one elder's wife was holding the child in her arms. The other elder's wife came to pick up her handbag from the church, but when she went outside, she found people shouting and praising God because the child woke up and started to play with the elder's wife who was holding him. They all came back into the church some singing, some praying, and some shedding tears of joy. That day there was great celebration.

On 30 August 2012, I was able to trace the parents at Groombridge Sports Club where I was able to see the father and Blessmore, his elder sister and elder brother all who witnessed this incident. Blessmore is now nine years old and doing his grade three at Groombridge Primary School. Attached is his current photograph taken on 30 August 2012.

Blessmore and Sister Blessed Garawadya
Please see the other photograph of MR GARAWADYA and his children

The power of the name of Jesus Christ who died was buried and resurrected and ascended to heaven

Who can dispute that power?

Who Is the Holy Spirit?

The Holy Spirit is God, the third person of the Trinity. The Holy Spirit is a person, not force or energy field. He comforts, grieves, reproves, convicts, guides, teaches, and fills Christians. He is not the father or the son, Jesus Christ. He convicts humanity of sin and reveals Christ. He energises the church to withstand the devil.

Deception through Co-existence

From the above and all that I have been saying, it is conclusive that there is only *one God* who has revealed himself through Jesus Christ who was fully human and fully God. There is one God who is three distinct persons but one in essence. It is important, therefore, to know that any other world religion who do not believe that Jesus is fully God and the Messiah, Saviour of the world and have their belief system that is centred in their own writing apart from the Holy Bible are false. We are instructed by our Lord to separate ourselves from them.

There must never be any compromise or any acceptance or accommodation of such belief systems. It is the devil who as a policy is propagating acceptance and tolerance of world religions. God says that we must 'come out of them'. But the devil says let's join because he knows on the part of Christians there will be spiritual defilement. The church in general worldwide has lost its power and is now operating as a carnal institution and has tolerance of evil among its ranks because of these alliances with the devil-controlled organizations.

New World Order is not godly; it is the devil's weapon to penetrate Christian ranks and dilute the pure doctrines. Earlier on I gave an example of water and raspberry. If you pour water in a jar of raspberry, you only increase quantity but you cannot change the colour, but if you pour just a bit of raspberry in a jar of water, the colour changes immediately. If you look closely, you can see the red raspberry as it goes down the jar leaving behind it red liquid. This is what the devil is aiming at. He wants a church that is not hot or cold but lukewarm, a church that is full of fear of being chased by the devil instead of a church that is filled with Holy Spirit, chasing devil, talking in tongues, heaven-bound, and victorious.

In some churches, he has succeeded by emphasis on Jesus and rejecting the Holy Spirit. Some emphasise Holy Spirit because they want power and play down Jesus. You have to take the gospel as a full package. God is one.

We hear these days of the world religions wanting to come together with Christians to form a body that will be the advisory body to the United Nations (UN) on religious matters. Whose policies will be adapted? When their groups meet and vote on an issue, Christians will be just one vote against many and the majority vote will be for a false religion advice to UN. The devil is setting up one world religion in preparation for rise of the Anti-Christ. For Christians to join such a group for the purpose of peace and co-existence is to give the devil the green light to control the UN and Christians as well. Remember, we are at war; we must be wise as serpents and harmless as a dove. We must watch out for such religions as, Marmonism, Jehovah's witnesses, unification church, Christian science, spiritualism, scientology, new age, Hinduism, Islam and Baha'I faith, African traditional religions (ATR), etc. These though their belief system seem to be different, they have one common serious belief that of rejecting Jesus as the Saviour of the world. On this issue, they will ensure that the Christian should not use the name Jesus Christ in the UN advising body but use the name God for all to co-exist. Yet we know the power of Christians is in the name of Jesus Christ. This is where the devil is leading the world to. A world where all people worship God in any way one feels like, trying to reach God from every corner of the world by any means. Christianity is God reaching out for the lost people and restoring relationship and reconciling people to himself. 'Do Not Be Yoked With Unbelievers'

Do not be yoked together with unbelievers. For what do righteousness and wickedness have in common?

Or what fellowship can light have with darkness? What harmony is there between Christ and Belial?

What does a believer have in common with an unbeliever? What agreement is there between the temple of God and idols? For we are the temple of the living God. As God has said,

'I will live with them and walk among them, and I will be their God, and they will be my people' (2 Cor. 6: 16)

No compromise with the devil. The fight is to the end till death. Let's allow the Holy Spirit to operate, direct, and lead us to our Saviour Lord Jesus Christ. Let's keep our eyes on Jesus Christ. Victory! Victory is certain! We are more than conquerors through him who died for us.

'Therefore, come out from them and be separate say the Lord.' (2 Cor. 6: 14-18)

May God Bless You

'Come Out from Them'

Amen!

BIOGRAPHY

Lukas Utete born second in a family of nine received his calling to ministry when he was a general sales manager of what was then, the biggest Coca-Cola Bottling Plant in Africa

Before going to Bible College, he was deacon in the Apostolic Faith Mission, AFM, in Zimbabwe church. As a Director of Evangelism, he went around Zimbabwe and went as far as Zambia and Mozambique with the team he led preaching the Gospel of Jesus Christ and Discipling Converts.

At the time when AFM in Zimbabwe sent its first missionary Rev. I. Magaya to Kenya, he was among the first people to be members of the Board of Trustees for Missions.

He was chosen to pastor a small group of people in Police and Prison officers' residential camps which used to meet for one and a half hours on Sundays. At the time he left for Bible College in 1997, the group had grown to 150 people and still growing and was then an elder in the church. He was requested to carry on pastoring that church during his college years. He did his Diploma in Theology and holds a BA degree.

At the time the book was published in 2003, he was ordained and still pastoring the church which had grown to 286 members.

He is the Director of Publicity and Information and a Lecturer at Living Waters Bible College. He is married to his beautiful wife Maria and the two have four children: two boys and two girls, all now married. Author has eight grandchildren.

Are You Not Deceived?

END NOTES

1. Tim o'Hagan, *Practical Problem Solver* (Capetown: The Readers Digest Association, 1994) p. 10.

2. Roy Gingrich, *The History of Satan* (Memphis Tennessee: Riverside Press Publishers, 1983) p. 3.

3. Hal Lindsey, *The Liberatiuon of Planet Earth* (Lakeland: Hunt Barnard Printing Ltd, 1974) p. 5.

BIBLIOGRAPHY

1. Johnson, Ron. *Lectures Notes.* Harare: Living Waters Bible College, 1999.

2. Lindsey, Hal. *The Liberation of Planet Earth.* Lakeland: Hunt Barnard Printing Ltd, 1974.

3. Mcdowell, Josh. *Evidence that Demand a Verdict.* Amersham-on-the-Hill: Nutprint Ltd., 1972.

4. Murefu, Constantine. *Lectures Notes.* Harare: Living Waters Bible College, 1999.

5. O'Hagan, Tim. *Practical Problem Solver.* Capetown: The Readers Digest Association.